books
BO
www.b

Bee Three Publishing is an imprint of Books By Boxer
Published by
Books By Boxer, Leeds, LS13 4BS UK
Books by Boxer (EU), Dublin D02 P593 IRELAND
© Books By Boxer 2023
All Rights Reserved
MADE IN CHINA
ISBN: 9781915410146

MIX
Paper | Supporting
responsible forestry
FSC™ C007683

This book is produced from responsibly sourced paper to ensure forest management

NEW HAT BOOBS

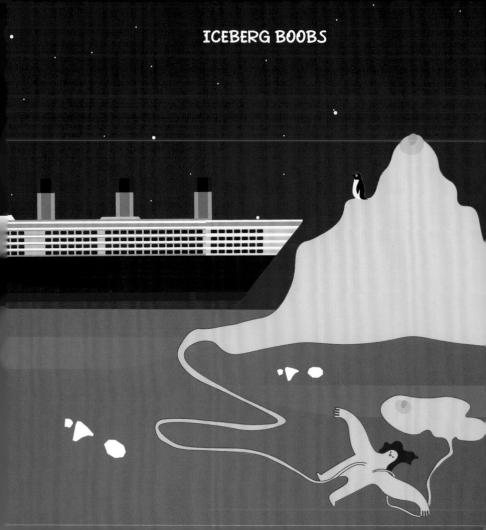

KING KONG BOOBS

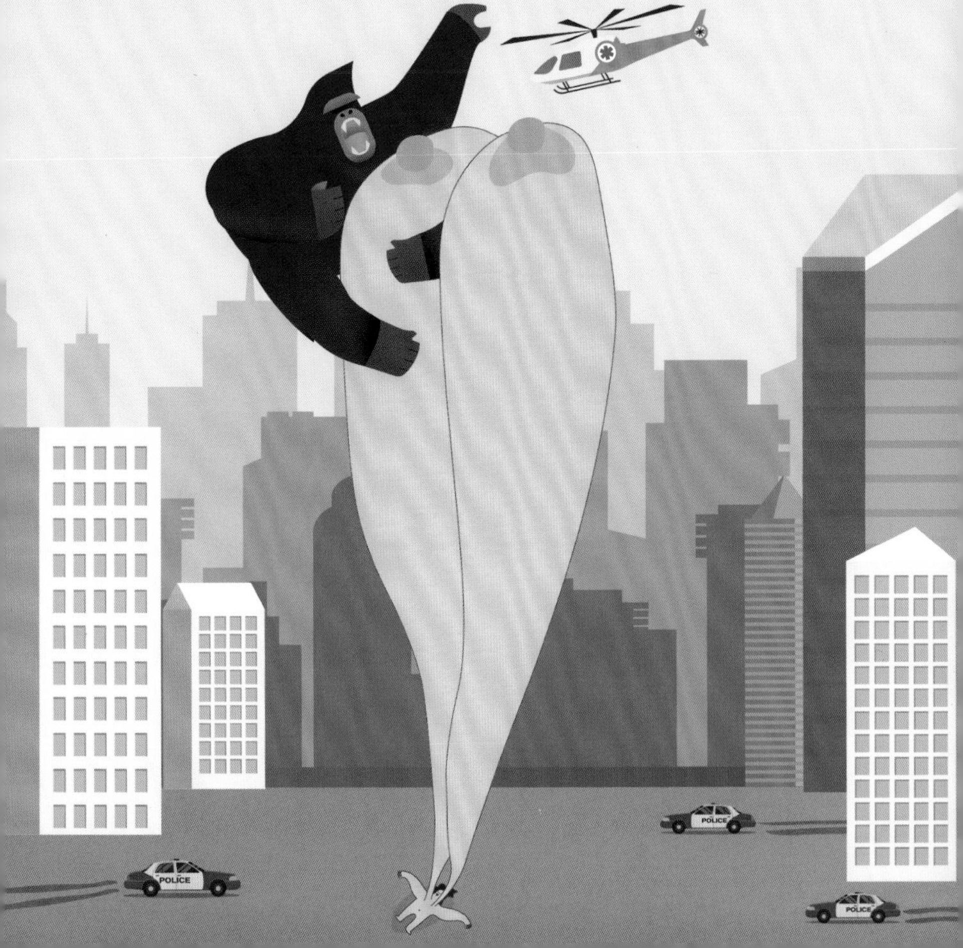

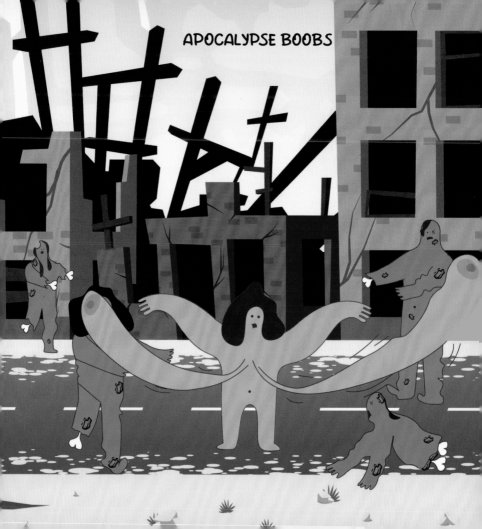

SURFBOARD BOOBS

LIFEBOAT BOOBS

AIRBAG BOOBS

BOUNCY CASTLE BOOBS

BUNGEE JUMPING BOOBS

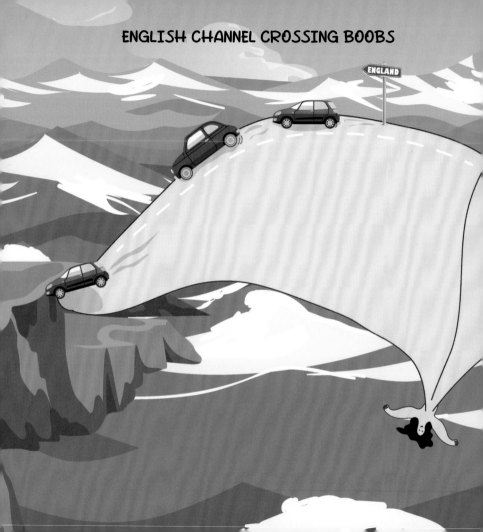

BURGER FLIPPING BOOBS

BUTTERFLY CATCHING BOOBS

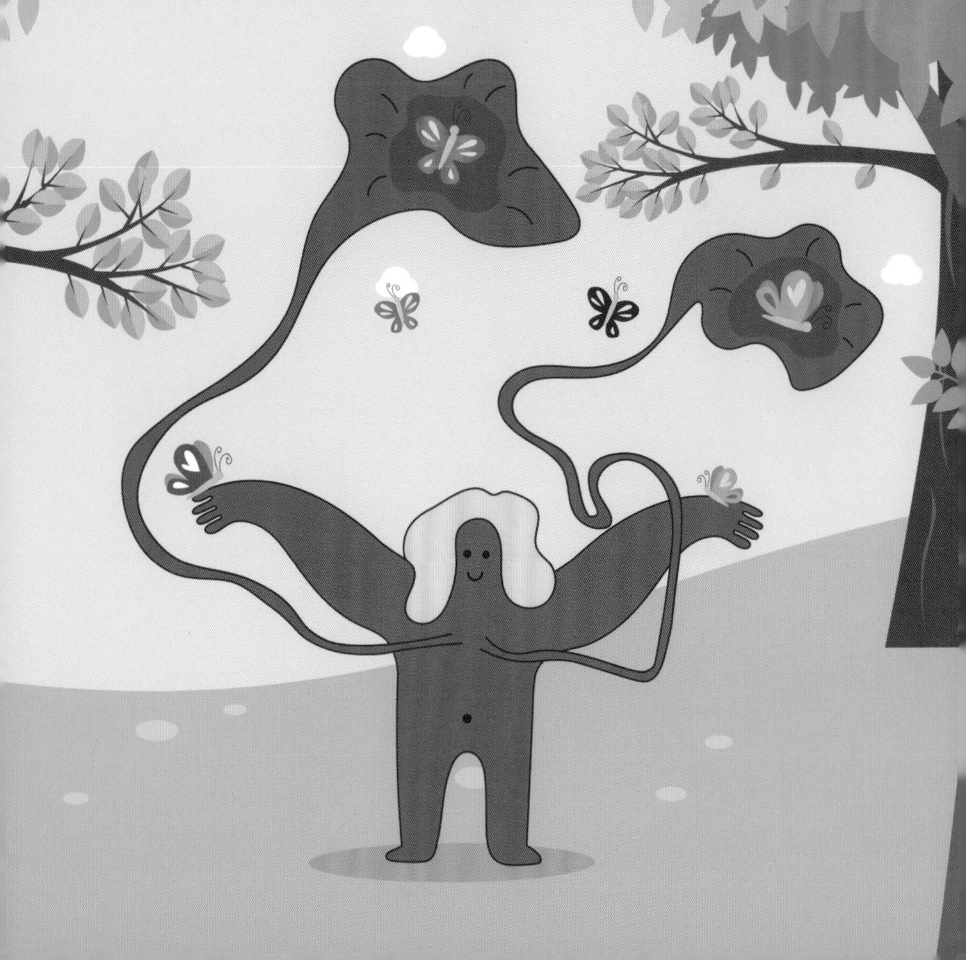

CATAPULT BOOBS

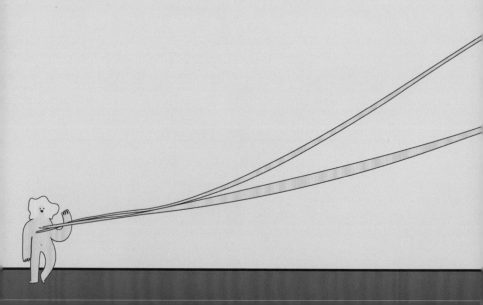

CHAIR BOOBS

CRASH BARRIER BOOBS

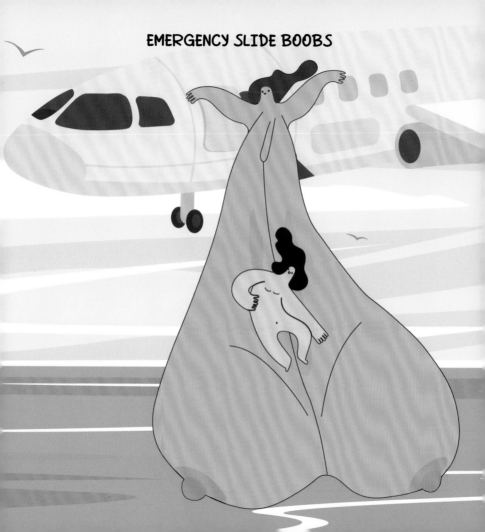

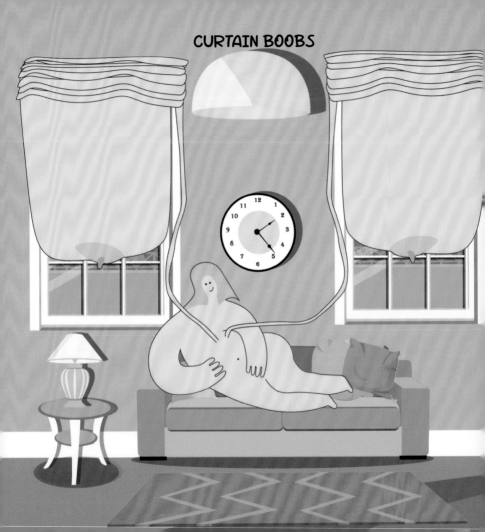

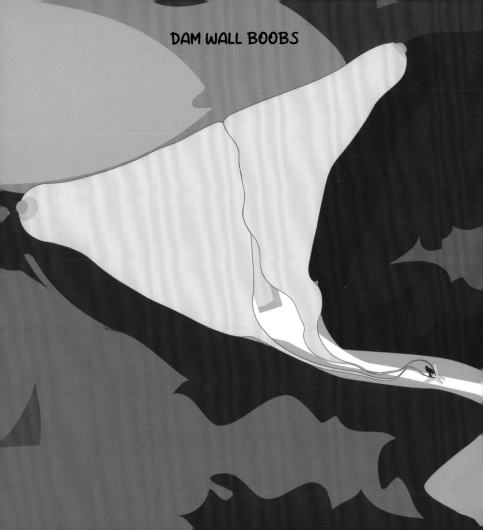

DRAUGHT EXCLUDER BOOBS

COMFORTER BOOBS

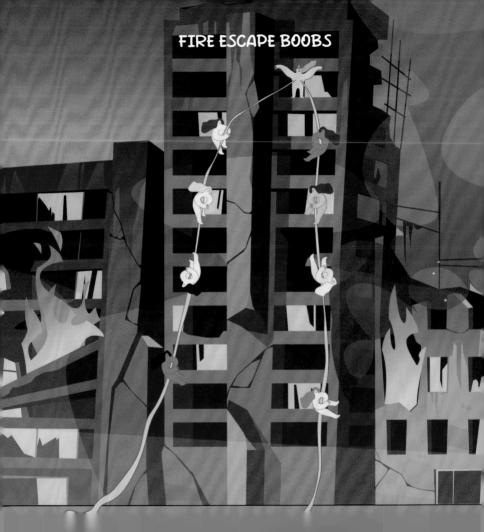

FISHING NET BOOBS

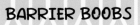

GRAND CANYON SWING BOOBS

GUIDING PLANES BOOBS

HAIR ROLLER BOOBS

HELICOPTER PROPELLER BOOBS

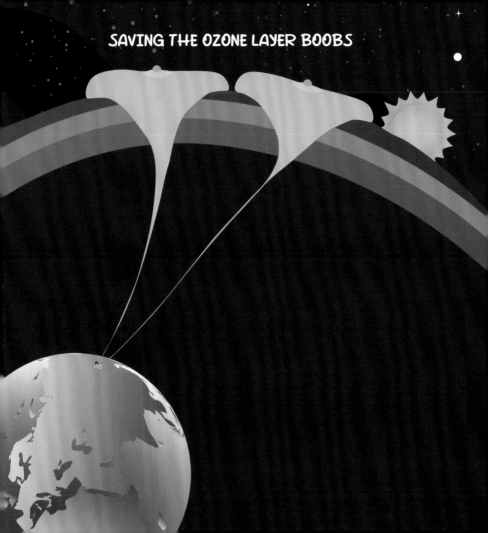

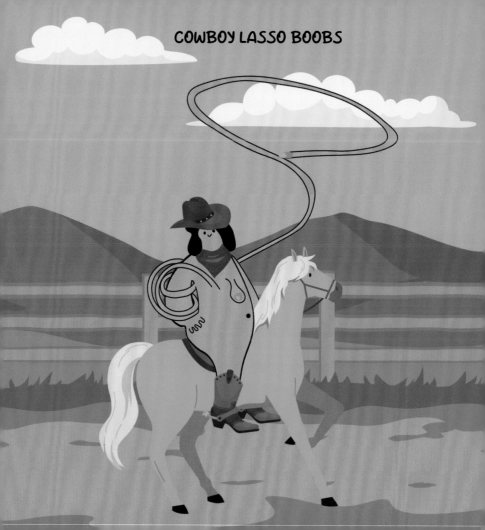

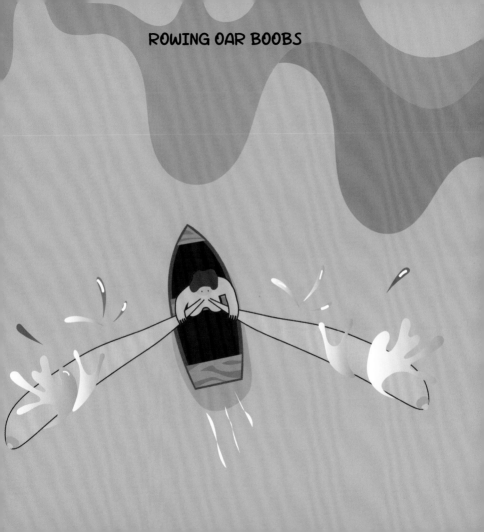

ROWING OAR BOOBS

MEASURING THE DISTANCE BETWEEN THE
EARTH AND THE MOON BOOBS

KEEPY-UPPY BOOBS

TYRE BOOBS

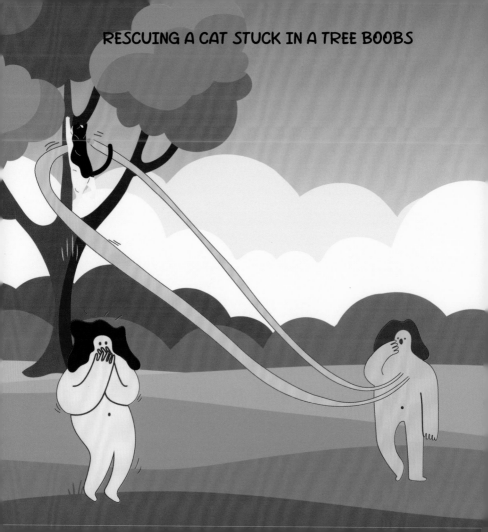

ROCK CLIMBING BOOBS

RUBBER RING BOOBS

ROLLERCOASTER BOOBS

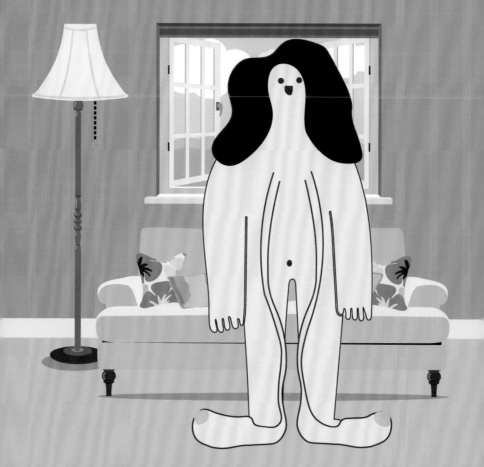

SPACE HOPPER BOOBS

DINING TABLE BOOBS

GROUP SELFIE BOOBS

TAPE MEASURE BOOBS

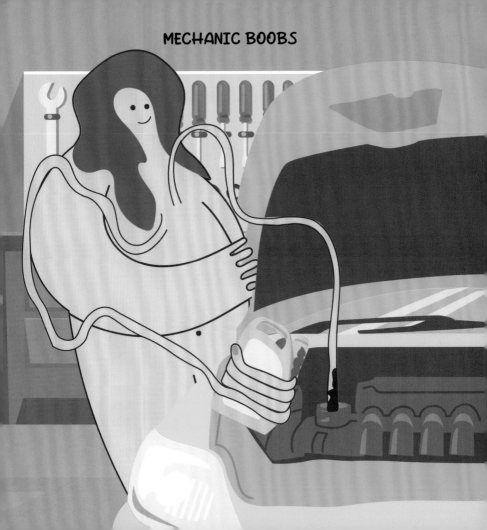

MECHANIC BOOBS

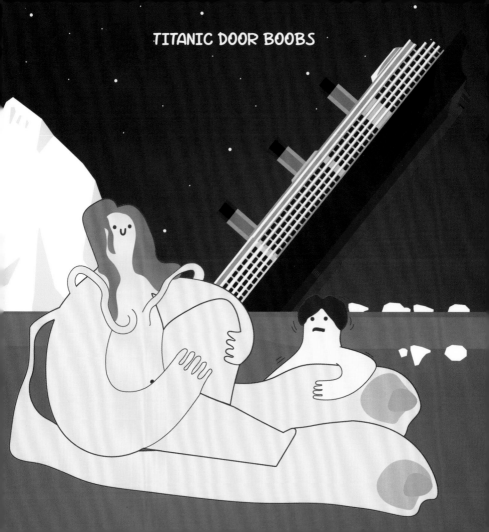

UMBRELLA BOOBS

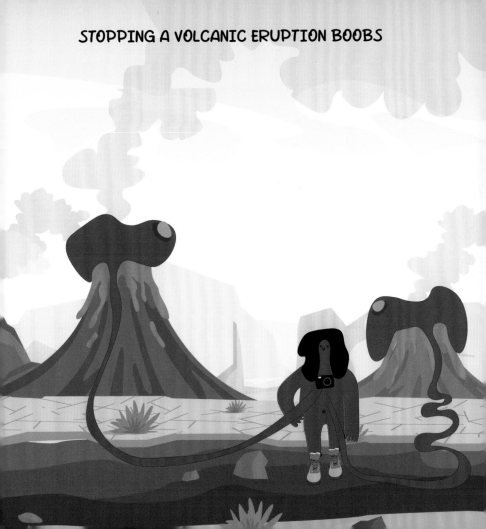

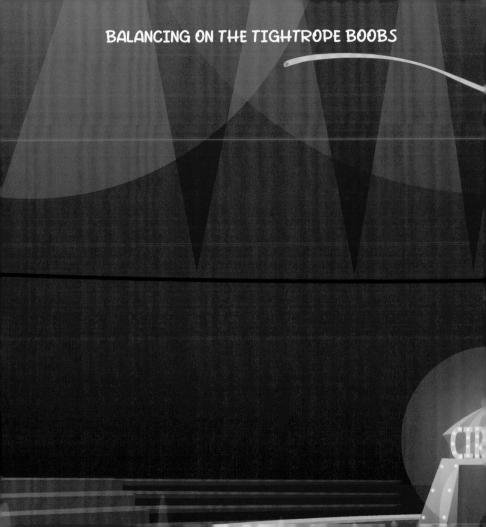

CIR

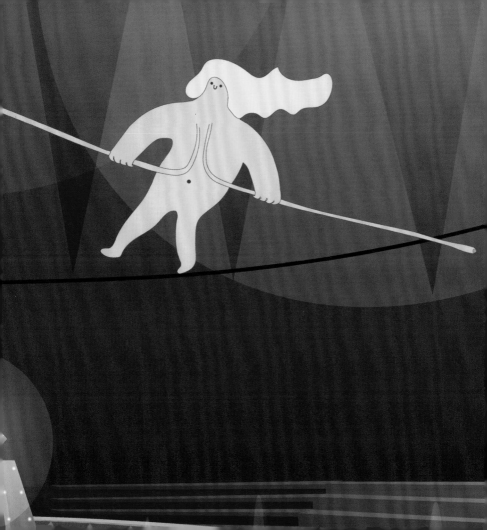

FETCHING WATER FROM A WELL BOOBS

WINDMILL BOOBS

WINDOW CLEANING BOOBS

ROAD BLOCK BOOBS

TUG-OF-WAR BOOBS

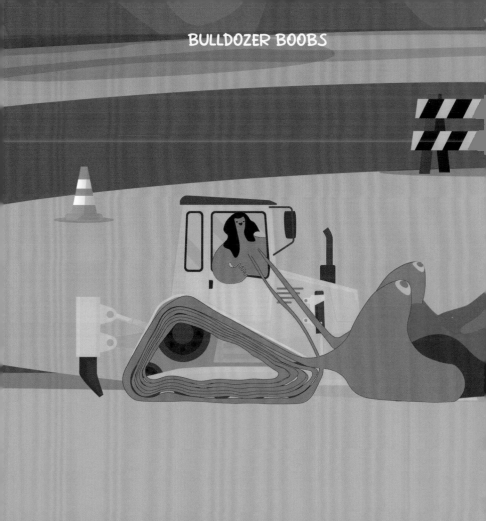

ZIP-LINE BOOBS

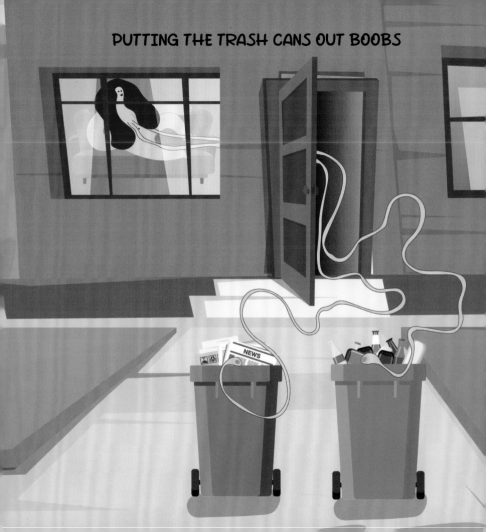

A NEW SETTLEMENT BOOBS

TUBE MAN BOOBS

MAKING A CUP OF TEA BOOBS

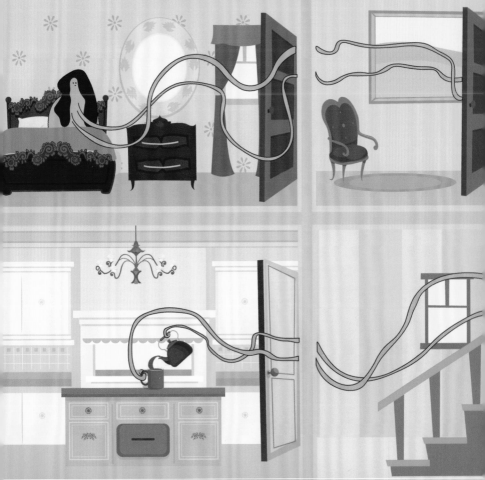

SUBMARINE BOOBS